GROWING FOOD IN WINTER

An Introduction To Growing Food Crops Out Of Season

By

James Paris

Published by

Deanburn Publications

Blog:

PlantersPost.com

Index

Introduction:

Many people have the belief that when the cold winter starts and the light fades quickly, the growing season comes to an end.

Thankfully this is not entirely the case.

Whilst it is certainly true that for the most part the winter period heralds the end of the main food growing season, there are still some vegetables and herbs that can be grown almost, if not all winter long.

The fact is that all plants need a certain amount of light and a minimum temperature before they will grow at all.

This tends to be a minimum of 6 hours daylight, and a minimum temperature of above 30F (-1c) before they will even survive, and higher still if we are to see any growth on the plant.

Fortunately there are a few ways that both these basics can be achieved by natural and 'mechanical' means – as I hope to lay out in this short work on the subject.

What is winter?

Although this might seem obvious, this is not an unreasonable question.

Winter in Florida for example is a world away from winter in Seattle.

Likewise a winter day in Australia would seem like a warm day out in the North of Scotland.

Some areas like USDA Zones 10-12 can be regarded as frost-free during winter, and so offer the potential for a larger variety of food plants that can be grown.

For this reason I will simply qualify winter thus…No matter where you live on the planet, winter for this book, is the coldest and darkest season of the year for you.

A time when growing vegetables or food plants seems like an impossible task.

For some regions winter is nothing to be afraid off. Many root vegetables will happily be left in the ground without any damage being done.

This is certainly the case in milder temperate zones that do not get deep penetrating frost.

Roots such as carrots, parsnip, turnips, for example can be left in the ground with just a covering of straw to protect against a mild frost – more on this later.

However cold winter temperatures will completely destroy soft fruits like tomatoes (yes tomatoes are a fruit!).

But winter is not all about the cold – it is also about the lack of sunshine hours or even just daylight.

So we have to look at plants that will grow with minimum daylight available – or look at ways to supplement the natural daylight with artificial.

With all that said, I do hope to give the reader some ideas not only for what food plants can be grown over winter, but also what will grow late into the season overall.

Also some guidance on winter garden preparation and storing food that can be eaten throughout the winter period.

So to begin with a look at the period just before winter proper sets in – the Autumn or 'fall' period.

Preparation for the Fall:

Preparing the vegetables for the Fall period really begins in the early summer with the planting out of vegetables that you hope to harvest late in the season.

This is to consider what vegetables can best survive as the winter approaches – and indeed thinking ahead as to how you will preserve them over winter.

Many vegetables actually benefit (or at least can survive) from a touch of frost, and these are **spinach**, garlic, leeks, broccoli, kohlrabi, kale, cabbage, carrots, chicory, brussels sprouts, corn salad, arugula, parsnip, fava beans, radish, mustard, and potatoes in the ground.

With root vegetables in particular such as carrots, turnips, and parsnips, these can be grown late into the autumn season.

As winter descends, they can be either picked and stored in a root cellar – more on this later – or they can be covered over in the ground with a mulch of straw or dry leaves to protect them from a surface frost.

If you are in a region where deep penetrating frost is the norm, then a root cellar is best for storing your late gravest.

To further highlight the Autumn season and what can be planted before true winter arrives, Some tips from my Fall Gardening Tip book…

Autumn Planting

Although the Autumn may be upon you and the fall has already started, in some areas there is still vegetables that can be planted for a late winter crop – this is especially so if you live in the warmer planting zones as indicated in the maps below.

For a clearer picture of the individual average temperatures, the following diagram makes things a lot clearer.

My apologies in advance to my readers from other parts of the world for only including the US & UK figures here, restricted as I am by expediency. A quick Internet search is all it takes however, to get the hardiness zones for your own country of residence.

Plant Hardiness Zone Map of the British Isles

°F	Zone	°C
0 to 5	7a	-15.0 to -17.7
5 to 10	7b	-12.3 to -14.9
10 to 15	8a	-9.5 to -12.2
15 to 20	8b	-6.7 to -9.4
20 to 25	9a	-3.9 to -6.6
25 to 30	9b	-1.2 to -3.8
30 to 40	10a	1.6 to -1.1

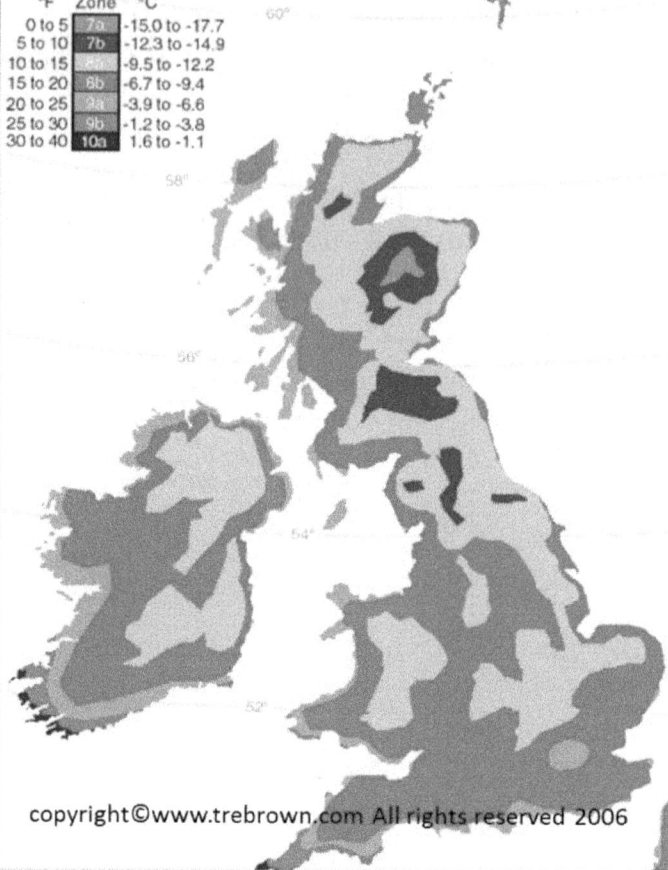

12

Autumn Crucifers (Brassicas):

Planting in the fall is possible with brassicas in the more southerly regions, mainly however the Fall is harvest time for these tasty veggies.

This **includes broccoli, winter cabbage, brussels sprouts** and cauliflower, all of which can do well in the fall and produce fresh vegetables over the Christmas season.

Indeed they thrive in the cooler temperatures of Autumn, and as an added bonus you will not be fighting off the cabbage moth as you would do over the summer season!

Seedlings should be started in late summer for an Autumn harvest, about 3 months before the first frost of winter.

Radishes are also a good choice for late planting as they will mature from seed in about 30 days. They are also able to withstand a light frost.

Carrots and parsnip take around 65 days to mature, and can be left in the ground if protected from ground frost.

This can be done simply by covering with mulching material, straw, or fallen leaves.

Late Autumn varieties such as 'Autumn King' can be planted as late as August and be ready for harvest by late October.

Lettuce is fast growing (about 30 days from seed). Choose a loose leaf variety so you are able to cut away leaves as you need them, rather than wait for a full head to form.

Garlic: If you're a garlic lover then this can be planted in the late fall in many zones for a late spring-early summer harvest. Protect from the worst of the winter by covering with loose straw or mulch.

As an aside – garlic is an excellent companion plant for carrots, as the pungent smell distracts the carrot fly!

Cover Crops:

Rather than leave the ground bare and unproductive over the late season/winter, try planting out some cover crops such as ryegrass, winter rye, white clover, sweet clover, crimson clover, hairy vetch and buckwheat.

Planting cover crops is a highly efficient way of improving the soil structure as well as adding nutrients and preventing soil erosion during exceptionally dry or wet periods.

Simply sow the seeds (usually before mid-August), and (after cutting if necessary) turn over the mature crops into the soil in the early spring.

Hardy Legumes such as Hairy vetch (Vicia villosa) make excellent nitrogen-fixing cover crops that provide organic matter as well as fertilizer. Sow in the Autumn and cut down before they flower in the early spring, then till them under.

Alternatively you can cover the growing area with leaf moult, or with the last of the summer grass cuttings. Leave to cover the area over winter, and turn into the ground before planting again in the springtime.

This is an efficient way to add humus and nutrients to the soil by using up the excess material that the Fall may produce.

Growing In Raised Beds?

Another thing to consider, is growing in raised beds. This extends your growing season, as the raised beds stay warmer for longer into the season.

This concept is particularly effective for root vegetables as the infill (if it has been done properly!) will be warm, loose and ideal for growing carrots and parsnips in particular.

If you have a poly-tunnel this also is perfect for growing later Autumn or early spring crops.

Storing Seeds/Planting Bulbs:

Collecting and storing your own seeds can save money and assure you of good crops in the next growing season. Tulip, crocus and daffodil bulbs can be planted at this time, not only for a beautiful back-drop, but also as an addition to your companion planting efforts.

Store your seeds by laying out on a shelf until they have dried out completely, then place into a brown paper bag over winter. Remember to label the bag clearly. I don't know how many times I have neglected to do this, and suffered the consequences when the planting season was suddenly upon me!

You may have to keep them in a sealed container in order to keep them away from rodents that will otherwise treat them as a healthy snack!

Harvesting & Storing Vegetables:

By the time that Fall comes around, many vegetables have not only been harvested already, but they have indeed been either consumed or made into pickles, frozen or otherwise preserved for consumption over the cold winter months.

This is certainly the case for tomatoes, cucumber, zucchini and other soft vegetables (ok, so tomatoes are actually a fruit I know!).

However there are a few vegetables that actually do best harvested in the colder weather of late Autumn, and these include most of the root vegetables such as carrots, parsnips, beetroot and swedes.

Other crops such as broccoli, cauliflower, brussels sprouts and winter cabbage should be ready to harvest before Christmas, and stored for the festive season in particular (is there any other time where kids will eat brussels sprouts!).

Onions at this time should be pulled up and laid on the ground to dry, before hanging up in the garden shed or other cool, frost-free environment.

Listed below are some of the most common vegetables that are harvested/stored during the Fall season.

Brussels Sprouts:

These are best harvested after a light frost, and this is done by starting at the base of the stem and snapping away the small sprouts.

The sprouts lower on the stem will mature first, and a few days later be followed by those higher up. Generally the sprouts will be ready to harvest about 80 days after planting, and are best harvested during cold weather.

Sprouts can last for 2-3 weeks if kept in the refrigerator, preferably in a container lined with kitchen towel to prevent sweating.

They also freeze well after blanching and will last this way for several months.

Broccoli:

Broccoli should be picked when the head is good and firm, and before it begins to flower. Even if the heads or florets are small, they should be cut away before the flowers begin to show otherwise they will become inedible.

Although broccoli can be grown throughout the season, they prefer the cooler climates and should even be harvested in the morning before the sun warms the ground up for best flavour.

It is best eaten within a few days of plucking, but will last for 2-3 weeks in the fridge or a cool place. To keep for longer, then blanch for a few minutes before freezing.

Broccoli will keep for up to 1 year frozen.

Cauliflower:

Cauliflower is another cool-season crop that dislikes temperatures over 60F.

When the head has fully formed (meaning that it is compact and white) and it is ready to harvest, cut at the base of the head with a sharp knife, leaving some leaves intact to protect the head.

If the head has a course rough appearance, or is discoloured then it should be disposed of. Small heads that have started to open should also be harvested immediately as they will soon open completely and be inedible.

It will keep in the refrigerator if wrapped in a polythene bag for about a week. To keep longer than this then it will have to be blanched and frozen.

Cauliflower also makes a good pickle, and will keep for several months in a pickle jar.

Cabbage:

Although cabbage is generally harvested and eaten before the Fall arrives, there are some winter cabbage varieties such as Huron, OS Cross and Danish Ball Head, that will last well into early winter.

These can be kept in the ground until ready to consume, so long as you are not in an area prone to severe frost or winter conditions that will result in the plant being burst and ruined.

If you do have to harvest to avoid the worst winter, then these cabbages are best kept in the cool environment of a root cellar.

There or in a refrigerator, they can last for several months stored on racks with a free flow of air around them.

Peas & Beans:

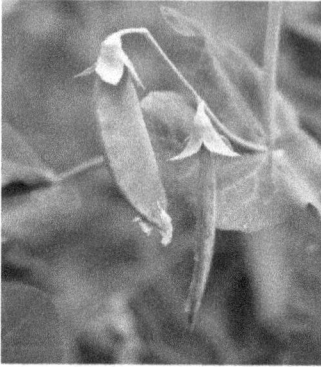

Now is the time to bring in the last of the pea and bean harvest – again depending on the varieties you have planted.

Peas and beans can be kept frozen for up to 12 months by simply removing them from the pods, then blanching for about 90 seconds in boiling water before cooling then freezing them.

Alternatively they can be dried out and stored for months to be used in soups and casseroles. This can be done either by leaving then on the plant to mature and dry out, or by removing the beans from the pod and laying them out in well ventilated place to dry completely.

If leaving on the vine to dry, then freeze for a minimum of 48 hours after harvesting to kill any bean weevils that may be present.

This process will kill the eggs, larvae and any adult weevil that may have infected the bean whilst on the plant.

Leeks Onions & Shallots:

Late onions and shallots should be pulled from the ground and left for a few days to dry out – unless of course the weather has turned wet in which case you should lay them out on racks indoors where it is cool and dry.

After the foliage has dried then they should be strung together and hung up somewhere cool, dry, and frost-free for the winter.

In this condition they will last for several months over winter, usually until the following springtime.

Leeks on the other hand like colder climates and can be left in the ground over winter, provided that you do not have a deep penetrating frost.

To protect them from deep frost, mulch over them with straw or dry grass up to 10 inches or so deep. They can then be lifted as and when they are needed.

To store above ground, they will keep in the fridge for about 1 week as they are lifted and cleaned. Alternatively cut the greenery away to about 1 inch above the white, leave the roots intact and store in box with damp sawdust or vermiculite.

Stand the plants upright and store away in a root cellar preferably, where it should be cool and moist. They will keep fresh for up to 8 weeks or so in this condition.

Root Vegetables:

Root vegetables are fairly versatile when it comes to harvesting, owing to the fact that they can often be left exactly where they are in the ground!

This is especially the case with parsnips and swedes which can benefit from a light touch of frost. If you are in an area that is prone to deep ground frost however they are best harvested and stored.

To 'store' them over winter in the ground, they must be treated pretty much the same way as the leeks in the previous chapter, with a protective covering of straw or mulching material.

Do not worry about a covering of snow, as this only acts as an insulator for ground-dwelling root vegetables.

If you are lifting them and storing them for the winter, then roots such as carrots, parsnips, swedes, potatoes and beets must be kept in a humid but well-ventilated frost-free area.

The high humidity (around 85-90%) acts to prevent the vegetables from drying out, giving that wrinkled look you so often see when veggies are stored inside.

The ventilation is to prevent the growth of fungal contaminants that would otherwise prosper is a damp environment.

There are several very effective ways to store your root vegetables, that will keep them fresh and crisp over the winter months ahead.

Vegetable Clamp:

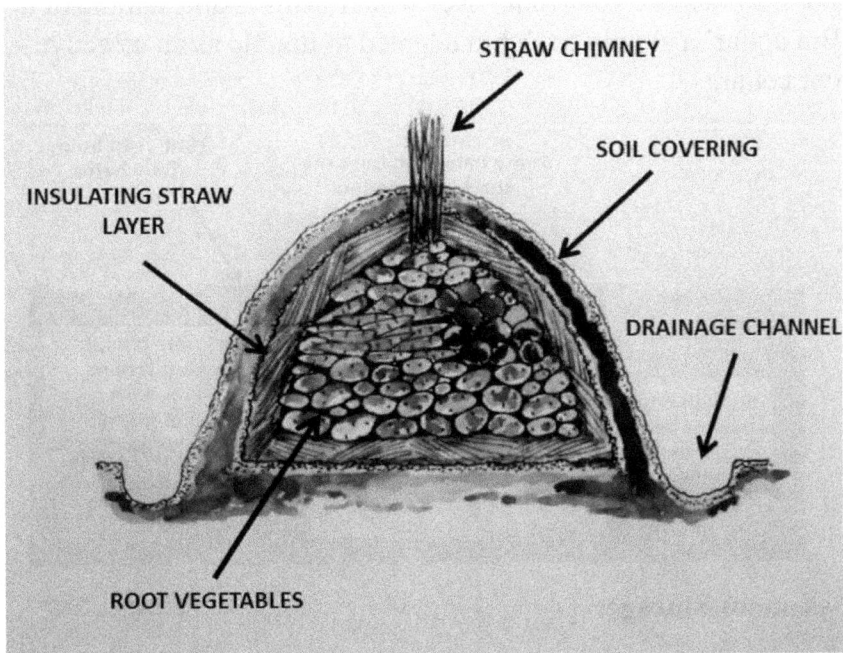

STRAW CHIMNEY

SOIL COVERING

INSULATING STRAW LAYER

DRAINAGE CHANNEL

ROOT VEGETABLES

In the illustration above you can see the simple layout of the root clamp. This should be constructed on a slight raise in the ground if possible, on free-draining soil to prevent water from gathering amongst the vegetables.

A small 'moat' is formed around the mound and filled with crushed gravel to act as drainage. The Roots are laid out on a bed of straw, covered over with a 2-4 inch layer of straw, then covered over again with about 6 inches of garden soil (thicker if you have severe winters).

You will notice a bunch of straw poking out of the top? This is to act as ventilation for the vegetables stored below.

Bin Cellar:

Many types of every-day articles can be buried under the ground and used to store your roots over winter. This is an example of a 'Bin cellar' a simple trash bin adapted to double as an effective root cellar.

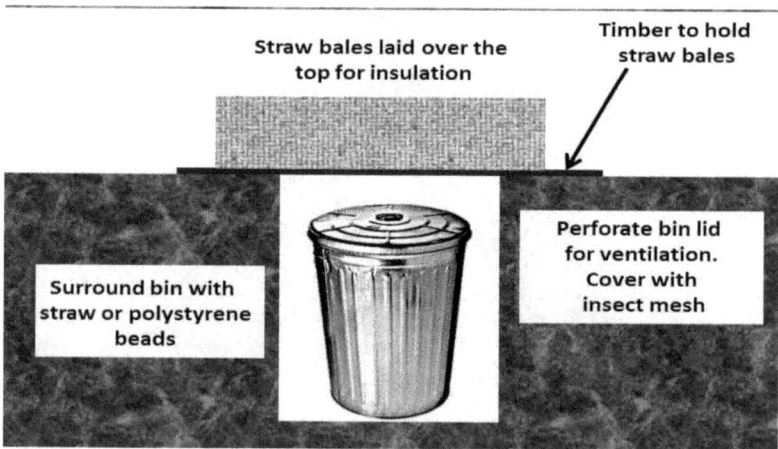

Straw bales laid over the top for insulation

Timber to hold straw bales

Surround bin with straw or polystyrene beads

Perforate bin lid for ventilation. Cover with insect mesh

Basement Storage:

If you happen to have a basement or even a garden shed adapted to make it frost-free, then roots can be simply stored in shallow boxes or crates.

Before storing carrots, parsnips or beets; cut or twist away the foliage to about 1 inch from the top. Be careful especially with the beets that you do not damage the beet itself, or it is likely to 'bleed out.'

Lay out your box then add an inch or so of moist sand or sawdust, before laying out a layer of carrots or parsnips. Fill over with the moist filler before adding another layer of roots. Continue this process making sure that the vegetables do not touch.

Potatoes can be simply stored in a dark place in the corner, then covered over with hessian or paper sacks.

Permanent Root Cellar:

Of course the ideal solution for storing beets over-winter, and fruit, vegetables, and dairy products over the summer periods, is a full-blown Root Cellar!

The remit for building such a Cellar is a bit beyond the intentions of this short work on vegetable storage, however the basic principle is the same as that of the 'Bin' cellar in that you are aiming for a high relative humidity, a frost-free environment and good ventilation.

Food Crops that Actually Grow in Winter

It has to be admitted from the outset that the range of food crops that can **actually be grown** over a cold winter are very limited – and in most cases impossible.

As mention in the previous examples, **most 'winter crops' are actually crops that can be grown late Autumn and at least partially harvested in the early winter.**

In effect, they do not actually 'grow' or at best have stunted growth over the winter period - Unless of course you are growing them under cover!

A polytunnel or 'hoop-house' is really the best way to consider growing anything over the cold winter.

And even then, some modifications will have to be made for the coldest part of the season.

First of all, what food crops can be grown over the winter – even in a Polytunnel?

Apart from what may be already on the plant such as the brussels sprouts mentioned earlier, winter crops consist of leafy greens or salads in the main.

A list of winter greens that you could grow in a Polytunnel would include…

Pea shoots: You cannot grow them to pods in winter, but pea shoots are an excellent nutritional source and look great on salads.

A good winter shoot variety would be the Meteor or the Austrian winter pea.

Winter lettuce will grow well under cover over the winter, and provide you with fresh leaves on a regular basis.

A good winter lettuce variety would be 'Density' and 'winter king'.

Mustard leaves are quick and easy to grow, and add a real spiciness to any salad dish. Plant in small rows just 1 week or so apart to give a regular crop of this salad plant.

Beetroot greens are another good food crop to grow in the Polytunnel as they are a hardy plant that can survive low temperatures near freezing.

The leaves and stems are colourful and substantial, even without the actual 'beet' and a valuable addition to the winter food crop.

Most popular beet varieties like 'Detroit Dark Red' can be grown for leaves throughout the winter under cover.

Spinach varieties such as Corvair,' 'Kolibri,' 'Auroch,' and 'Space,' can be planted late Autumn and harvested throughout the winter.

Spinach is a huge source of iron over the winter months, packing high amounts of carotenoids, vitamin C, vitamin K, folic acid, iron, and calcium – and it tastes great!

Winter purslane is a small heart-shaped leaf that is similar in taste to spinach, and can be grown and picked right through the winter months under cover.

Lambs lettuce is another fast-growing salad leaf, but this can also be blanched or partially cooked and served as a vegetable with the main meal.

It is a delicate plant with a mild nutty flavour and can be grown all winter long in a covered area.

Purple Mizuna is often found in the supermarket salad mix. This is easily recognizable because of its serrated leaves. It is quick to grow and can be cooked or eaten fresh in a salad.

Salad Burnet is another quick growing salad plant. Best used by picking the young shoots as it becomes slightly tough and bitter as it grows.

Trim no more than a third of the plant at any time if you want it to supply new shoots throughout the winter.

Swiss Chard is a 'hardy' winter crop and will grow slowly provided it gets adequate light and is protected against the hardest frost.

An amazing colourful vegetable, great for stir fry's.

Pak Choi is an excellent alternative to lettuce and even more versatile, as it can be cooked into a stir-fry for example.

A flavoursome vegetable, it is mainly grown as an end-of-season crop but will grow slowly over winter if it s protected from the frost.

Arugula has an interesting oak shaped leaf and a slightly nutty flavour, another popular plant in the supermarket salad mix packs.

It will grow throughout the winter if it is protected from the frost, and can be planted 2 weeks apart to give a regular supply.

Winter Herbs:

Cold-hardy herbs, such as chives, mint, oregano, parsley, rosemary, sage and thyme, can often survive cold winter temperatures, especially under the protection of a greenhouse or hoop-house.

They will grow slowly but overall continue to produce a good source for the kitchen over the winter period.

Microgreens:

Microgreens are the seedlings of popular herbs and veggies that are harvested before maturity. Pea shoots mentioned earlier are a popular microgreen found in salad mixes.

These miniature versions of the mature plant, tend to be packed with flavor and are now regarded as a valuable addition to the kitchen table.

Another practical benefit is that microgreens can be grown in a wide variety of containers, and can be placed on a window sill or conservatory without taking up lots of space.

Other popular microgreens that will grow over winter in the right covered conditions include…

- Arugula
- Beet
- Crest
- Collards
- Radish shoots

- Broccoli
- Kale
- Lettuce
- Mustard
- Nasturtium
- Pak Choi
- Red cabbage
- Sunflower

Nasturtiums are a favourite for chefs and gardeners alike, as they are an edible plant that is also a good companion plant for tomatoes.

Chefs love the flowers to stuff for recipes. The flowers and leaves make good edible decoration and the young plant is a popular microgreen.

Food Crops that Over-Winter well.

There are many 'main crop' food varieties that over-winter well. By this I mean that they can be planted in the late summer and harvested right through to the Spring in some cases.

These varieties can be found in the earlier section on Autumn planting, but as a quick guide include the following (cold weather varieties)…

Brassicas: Also called "cole crops" or "crucifers," these include kale, cabbage, broccoli, cauliflower, Asian cabbages, mustard greens, Brussels sprouts, radishes, turnips, kohlrabi.

It should be noted that the cauliflower, and Asian cabbages like bok choy do need protected against hard frost.

Root vegetables are incredibly hardy but do not like hard-frozen ground. That aside, carrots, beetroot, parsnips and swede can actually benefit from a light frost.

Alliums such as leeks, onions and shallots can be left outside in the winter months especially if you protect them from the worst of the weather.

For a more complete explanation. Here is a preview of how to grow and care for Autumn or Winter food plants extracted from my book 'Gardening Tips For Winter'

Winter/Autumn Vegetables

When we talk about growing winter vegetables, it has to be made clear that unless you live in warmer climes then we are really talking about planting in the early fall, and reaping the benefits as the early winter progresses.

Alternatively they can be planted in the late spring, usually a couple of weeks before the last frosts, to be ready for harvesting before the warmer weather arrives.

The bottom line is that once temperatures start to drop below 35F then even hardy cool season seeds will not germinate.

Once the plant has germinated and is growing however, then it is a case of protecting it from sudden drops in temperature – especially in the evenings.

The two main categories of **cool season** vegetables we are talking about here are Hardy vegetables and semi-hardy vegetables.

All cool season crops taste better when they mature in the cooler weather , and are therefore best suited to planting in the late summer or early spring seasons.

Between them they will thrive in growing temperatures from 40F to 60F ideally. Warmer climates will generally cause them to bolt and become inedible, this is the case of beets and swedes especially.

Hardy Vegetables include - broccoli, cabbage, kohlrabi, onions, lettuce, leeks, peas, radish, spinach, turnips.

These veggies will grow in temperatures as low as 35-40F and will survive a light frost, especially if protected by a garden fleece covering.

Semi-Hardy Vegetables include - beets, carrots, cauliflower, parsley, parsnips, potatoes, and Swiss chard.

This type prefer temperatures above 45-50F but below 75-80F and are susceptible to very cold or frosty conditions.

It is not only the temperatures that restrict winter growth however, the shorter winter daylight hours mean that the plants may not get the minimum of 6 hours daylight required in most cases for garden vegetables.

The growing season of all vegetables and not just Hardy types can be extended considerably by the use of cold-frames, and polytunnels that will protect the plants against the worst of the winter weather.

Yet another way to extend the growing season or indeed protect vegetables from the coldest of weather is to consider Hot Bed gardening methods.

Hot Bed Gardening:

Although regarded by some as a 'new' concept in gardening methods (Is there such a thing?), this is an idea that goes way back in time – at least to the Roman conquest of Great Britain.

To supply the Roman generals with fresh salad in the frozen winters of Britain, was a challenge that the Roman gardeners of the time solved by using this method to supply fresh salad crops out of season – and probably stopped themselves getting flogged at the same time!

The French perfected this method in the early 1900's, and the Victorians used it to grow pineapples!

So what is it? A Hot Bed is basically an area heated by natural or artificial means to grow vegetables that would otherwise not grow owing to the cold temperatures.

There are quite a few ways to go about creating your own hot bed, here is one possible plan for a *natural* Hot Bed.

To create a simple Hot Bed garden you have to dig a trench 18-14 inches deep (450-600mm), then fill it with manure mixed with straw that has been piled up for 7-10 days beforehand. This is to allow a cooling down period otherwise the excess heat generated can kill the plants.

Once you have done this then place a cold-frame on top similar to the one below, and add 6 inches (600mm) good quality growing medium on top.

The heat generated will warm the soil, and the cold-frame arrangement will trap this heat nicely to allow growth and prevent frost in the cold season.

This natural method of Hot Bed gardening will on average last for about 3-4 months before the heat-producing aspect of the manure finishes.

The heat produced during this time should easily be in the region of 45-55F (8-13C) which puts it in the ideal range for the veggies listed below.

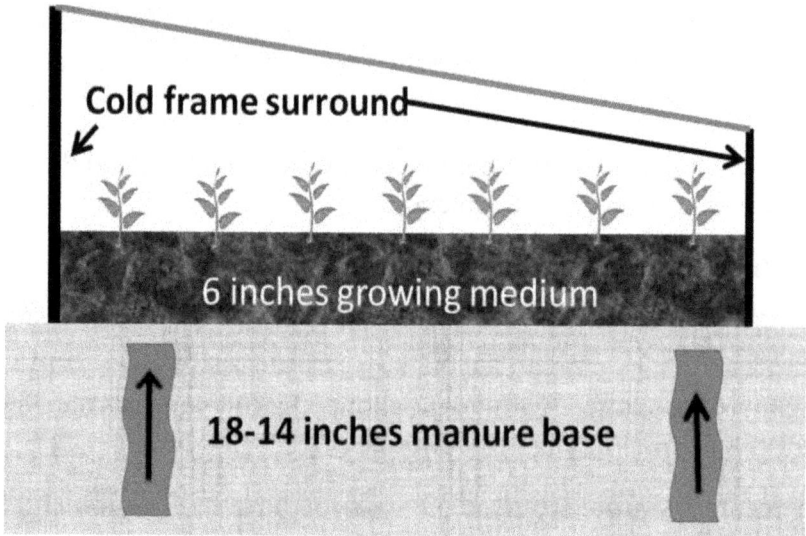

Cold frame surround

6 inches growing medium

18-14 inches manure base

Another alternative to this natural method is to utilise an under-soil electric blanket, or electric cables to warm the growing medium.

This will be more expensive to operate (unless you produce your own electricity?), however it is easier regulated and you will have heat for as long as you pay your electric bills :)

In general terms this method is used around January so that the timing is right for the early spring gardening. By March the effectiveness of the heating-up process has virtually gone (in the natural method), and 'normal' spring gardening practices take over.

However for growing winter greens this Hot Bed could be set up right at the end of the Fall or even into the winter cold period.

This would give your plants an excellent boost that will continue for many weeks into winter proper.

The good news is that you now have a nitrogen rich bed in which to grow a good variety of spring-summer vegetables (perhaps by removing the cold frame).

This may all seem like a load of extra work, however it is well worth considering if you are keen to keep your fresh vegetable supply going for as long as possible – even over the cold winter months.

You can also try a much simpler version by digging out the ground as above, but placing over it a mini-polytunnel to grow your veggies under.

NOTES/THINGS TO DO

NOTES/THINGS TO DO

Planting Times:

Normally when planting seedlings or from seed itself, it is important to consider the time it takes for the plant to reach maturity, or at least to become harvestable.

For instance planting too late in the Fall may mean that the plant will not reach maturity before the winter really closes in.

VEGETABLE	MINIMUM TEMP. F	OPTIMUM TEMP. F	APPROX. DAYS TO HARVEST
HARDY VEGETABLES			
BROCCOLI	40	80	65
CABBAGE	40	80	85
KOHLRABI	40	80	50
ONIONS (set)	35	80	65
LETTUCE (leaf)	35	70	60
LEEKS	40	80	120
PEAS	40	70	65
RADISH	40	80	30
SPINICH	40	70	40
TURNIP/SWEDE	40	80	50
SEMI-HARDY			
BEETS	40	80	60
CARROTS	40	80	70
CAULIFLOWER	40	80	65
PARSLEY	40	75	80
PARSNIPS	35	70	70
POTATOES	45	80	125
SWISS CHARD	40	85	60

Planting beets or swedes too late in the springtime may mean that the hotter weather will cause the plants to bolt and become inedible. With that in mind, here is a simple chart covering the growing times and required ground temperatures, for a selection of the most popular hardy vegetables you may consider for your winter veggies.

For winter planting however, this advice changes slightly as many of the growing conditions are going to be artificially created.

Indoor temperatures will be warmer than outside, and the lighting conditions possibly extended with artificial lighting.

That said, this is a good 'rule-of-thumb' temperature/harvest guide for popular veggies.

Another point to consider is whether or not you will be growing your vegetables under cover. As mentioned earlier, the use of a greenhouse, polytunnel, or cold-frame can mean that you are able to grow quite effectively in otherwise vegetable-intolerant conditions.

A polytunnel for instance that has perhaps been used to grow tomatoes during summer in cold northern regions, can be put to great use by growing a whole range of cool season vegetables.

Growing in Raised Beds is also an effective way to increase the growing season, as the Raised Bed tends to warm up quicker as it is lifted up from the cold ground temperatures of winter.

Combine the two and you have a marriage made in veggie heaven :)

Protecting Winter Vegetables.

Keeping your winter vegetables protected from the worst of the weather, is a no-brainer – especially after you have gone to all the bother planting them in the first place!

As mentioned earlier, this is considerably easier if you are growing your winter vegetables inside a polytunnel, cold-frame, or otherwise under cover.

Even in a polytunnel however, if the temperature drops below freezing it is advisable to cover your veggies with a gardeners fleece to protect against frost damage.

With vegetables growing outdoors, there are a number of precautions you can take to protect them from the worst of the weather.

For Parsnips and other root vegetables, providing the temperature does not fall below 23F (-5c) then they can effectively be left in the ground and covered over with a mulch of leaves or straw to a depth of around 6 inches.

There can be a downside to this method however, and that is that destructive pests and grubs can also use this method to over-winter in your veggie plot!

I overcome this problem by the following method. Wait till a few weeks before your last winter frosts, then (presuming you have harvested your vegetables by now) rake away the leaves and turn over the soil below with a garden fork.

This exposes any grubs and pests to the last of the frost and kills them. Alternatively, during this digging-over process you can include the leaf mulch into the soil, rather than removing it to add much-needed organic material.

This will not add much in the way of nutrients, as leaves are mainly carbon, but will improve the soil medium overall.

Do not worry too much about snow conditions, as snow acts as an insulator in most cases – protecting the veggies below. However if you are in an area that has severe penetrating ground frost, then it is best to harvest your root vegetables and store in a root cellar.

Alternatively store them in a sand-filled box in a garage or frost-free outbuilding.

Check out the diagram below for an example of a DIY ground-based root cellar.

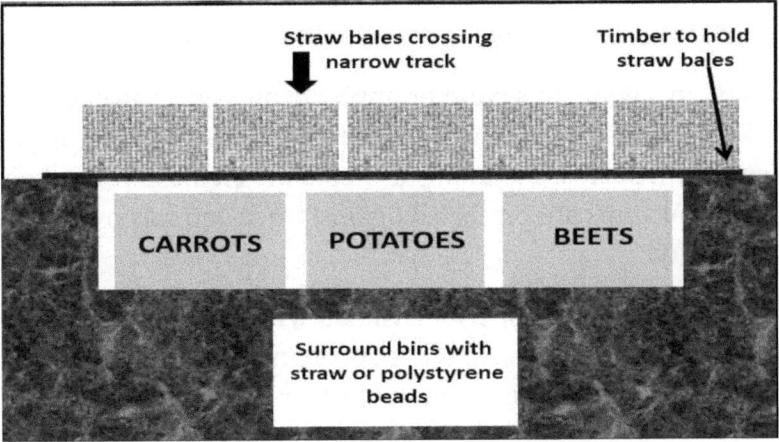

2. Garden fleece will protect your cool season vegetables such as broccoli, salad crops, or winter cabbage against frost damage. Fleece or netting will also protect them from the ravages of pigeons!

Even an old blanket or hessian sacking thrown over the veggies at night, will protect them from the night-time drop in temperature – just remember to remove it again in the daytime.

3. Leeks can be lifted before the ground is frozen and 'heeled in' to a trench that is sheltered from the worst weather. They will last several months over winter in this situation.

4. Vermin can do a lot of damage to vegetable crops left in the ground over winter – especially if the weather is particularly bad and food is at a premium.

A couple of years ago I lost a good parsnip crop that had been growing in pots & containers to a family of rats!

They dug the parsnips right down the length of the root to get every last morsel – I was gutted, as was my wife who had been looking forward to honeyed parsnips for the Christmas dinner!

Needless to say the rats were promptly dealt with, however I had to buy the Christmas parsnips. Use whatever means at your disposal to deny them access, including ½ inch chicken mesh if need be, to be sure your roots are protected against mice and rats over the winter period.

Rats in particular are opportunists, and will nest near a food source if they can find one. Make sure there are no easy places for them to set up home such as piles of junk or other rubbish.

Check out the compost heap regularly, as they will dig into the compost or piles of manure, for both the food source and the heat over winter months.

5. Build a cheap Polytunnel! This is not as hard as it might seem, and can be quickly achieved simply by bending plastic plumbers pipe into loops, and sticking the ends down into the soil.

Cover over with clear polythene, held down by soil along the length of the construction, and you have an instant – albeit a bit flimsy – polytunnel that will protect your plants admirably.

Here below is a picture of the same principle but covered with insect netting to protect against summer cabbage moth.

A Raised Bed vegetable garden offers even better possibilities as you can see from the picture below.

Just replace the insect mesh with either garden fleece or polythene to have a fully protected growing area for your Autumn/Winter vegetables.

Fresh winter vegetables can offer a valuable and nutritious change to dried or frozen vegetables. And even though you may certainly be restricted as to the choices open to you, there is no doubt that winter need not be completely unproductive when it comes to fresh veggies for the table.

NOTES/THINGS TO DO

My favourite Method For Growing Winter crops

Without a doubt, the best way to grow food over winter is under the cover of a Polytunnel or Greenhouse.

This will allow the most natural light whilst providing a covered area that you can prepare in such a way to keep out the worst of the cold.

I am fortunate enough to have a 30 foot Polytunnel where over the winter period I can grow a good range of crops such as the ones previously described.

I grow all my crops in shallow 6 inch deep raised beds for the most part.

These are covered over with horticultural fleece to protect against the frost and general cold air – and it works very well.

If I really want to give my plants a boost, I will use an electric blanket to encourage early growth in the Spring.

Otherwise I will use the Hot Bed technique discussed earlier, if I can get my hands on some fresh horse manure from the local stables.

Some Handy Tips:

Here are a few handy tips for growing winter veggies, some of which fly in the face of conventional growing methods.

Watering Issues. Contrary to brisk Summer growth, in the winter plants are very slow growing overall and need little in the way of water.

Water sparingly so that the ground does not become water-logged. Remember that the plant is not nearly as thirsty, nor is the temperature warm enough to leech away the water as it would in the summer.

Watering is also best left to the mid-morning period when the outside temperature has maybe raised slightly and the plant more active.

Leaving watering to the evening means that the water is more likely to freeze overnight and chill the plant.

The water must also be kept from the leaves if possible to prevent the water freezing and 'burning' the leaves.

This is best done by using a trickle-feed system where the water just goes to the roots of the plant, thereby avoiding frost damage.

Also another handy tip is to keep the water at 'room temperature' so that you do not shock the plant with freezing water when you do water it.

Watering with freezing cold water will result in stunted or slow growth overall.

Keep the water barrel inside the polytunnel and protected from frost with straw or horticultural fleece if you want to improve your chances of a winter crop.

Lighting Issues:

One of the main disadvantages that winter planting has apart from the cold, is the lack of daylight hours – especially bright sunshine.

Most plants need a minimum of 6 hours good daylight to thrive and prosper!

With the short winter days this is not possible so to encourage more plant growth artificial light can be brought into the 'equation'.

Even by just adding a couple of extra hours artificial light, you will increase your potential for a good winter growing season substantially.

What kind of light do you use for plants in the winter?

The most popular winter lights are the **Fluorescent lights.** These are an economical and easy choice to use.

Available in tubes or compact bulbs (CFL) that screw into regular lamp sockets, they are cool enough to put close to plant foliage.

When buying fluorescent tubes, look for "full-spectrum" or use a mix of "cool" and "warm" bulbs.

As for the choices of light type…

Fluorescent lights are an effective supplement to natural (window) light, and possibly the most popular choice.

High-Intensity Discharge (HID) lights are ideal for growing maturing edible plants, whilst Light-Emitting Diode (LED) lights are an excellent choice for efficiently growing large numbers of plants.

Heating/Insulation Issues:

When growing in winter I make the polytunnel as efficient as I can with regard to heat loss.

This means covering the inside with a bubble-wrap polythene to restrict heat loss, and restrict frost damage.

If you are growing in a Polytunnel, then consider the latest thermal polythene. This will not only be a good idea for winter planting, but is also effective over the summer months for reducing condensation in the inside of the tunnel.

Loosely covering the plants with bubble-wrap or horticultural fleece as mentioned earlier will massively improve your chances of a good harvest.

Likewise creating a 'hot bed' either with natural or artificial means will boost productivity.

Keep any cold draughts at bay by sealing up leaking door and windows with tape, or stuffing crack with fleece.

No-one – including your plants – likes a cold draught on a winters night!

Consider an outside heat source in the coldest weather.

There are many different electric greenhouse heaters available at reasonable cost that will at least keep the frost at bay – which is all you need for this exercise.

In the past, I have even used a paraffin lamp in a small covered area to good effect.

Preparing For Winter

As any gardener knows, preparation is at the 'root' of all success in the garden.

And this is indeed the case if you have any ambitions to grow food crops over winter.

Listed below is an 'action plan' that covers some of the most important tasks to do if your winter growing season is to be successful.

Tools & Equipment

Keeping the garden equipment in good shape is not always easy over a busy growing season. However this is an ideal winter task that will reap benefits in later months.

This is especially the case for the winter grower, as the last thing you want is to spread disease or infestation into your winter growing area.

The good thing here is that your winter plants will not have to put up with the onslaught of pests such as greenfly or cabbage moth.

However there are other pests and viral diseases that can overwinter in your newly-formed mild environment if you allow them to.

Squash vine borers, Colorado potato beetles, cabbage maggots, leaf cutter grub and cucumber beetles, are good examples of pests that will burrow into the ground to seek protection over the winter.

So be sure to thoroughly clean the garden tools and equipment – including any trellis etc – before bringing into the area.

Clean off your summer tools, especially secateurs and shears, pruners and loppers. Remove muck and rust then wipe them over with an oily rag. Do this before hanging up or packing away for the winter and you will be ready to go, perhaps after a quick sharpening in the spring.

Spades, shovels, garden forks etc should have the handles in particular checked and fixed if need be, before cleaning and hanging up to store.

Check over winter equipment. Late autumn is the time to check over any equipment you will need to see you over the winter. This would include heating and lighting in particular.

If you are using cloches for cover over your raised beds – even within the polytunnel – now is the time to see that they are in good condition and ready to use.

Get a few bales of straw if you are caring for outside root vegetables. Straw is an excellent insulator for both inside the Polytunnel or out in the veggie plot.

Scatter a layer 4-6 inches deep to protect plants from the frost and icy wind.

CONCLUSION

Patience is a virtue!

Patience will always play a large part with any successful garden. Unless you are growing mushrooms – plants just take time to mature!

When planting and growing over winter however, patience must be called on even more.

The fact is that unless you are forcing plants on with artificial light and heating, your average winter growth will be less than half of what you could expect when conditions are ideal.

Sometimes in the extreme, plants will cease to grow altogether and go into survival mode until the worst has passed.

This is to be expected, especially if you are not using artificial means to create ideal growing conditions.

In addition to the general information in this book, you may notice that I have included several pages with '**NOTES/THINGS TO DO' at the top?**

The secret of many good gardeners is that they keep good notes!

Please use these pages to record your success & failures 9we all get them) for future reference and to improve your chances of better results going forward.

Authors Thanks

Thanks a lot for purchasing this book – I really appreciate it!

You can find lots more vegetable gardening tips & advice at my blogsite.

PlantersPost.com

NOTES/THINGS TO DO

NOTES/THINGS TO DO

NOTES/THINGS TO DO

NOTES/THINGS TO DO